Permafrost

poems by

Gary V. Powell

Finishing Line Press
Georgetown, Kentucky

Permafrost

This book is dedicated to my wife, Mary, my constant inspiration, muse, and companion, my son, Sergeant Reilly Wilson Powell, who serves with the 75th Army Ranger Regiment, and my daughters, Jessica, the smartest English teacher in Omaha, and Ashley, the best mom in Winona.

Copyright © 2023 by Gary V. Powell
ISBN 979-8-88838-237-0 First Edition
All rights reserved under International and Pan-American Copyright Conventions. No part of this book may be reproduced in any manner whatsoever without written permission from the publisher, except in the case of brief quotations embodied in critical articles and reviews.

ACKNOWLEDGMENTS

"Perfume" was selected as an honorable mention for the Steve Kowit Prize and appeared in the 2020 *San Diego Annual*.

Publisher: Leah Huete de Maines
Editor: Christen Kincaid
Cover Art: istock.com
Author Photo: Mary Wilson
Cover Design: Elizabeth Maines McCleavy

Order online: www.finishinglinepress.com
also available on amazon.com

Author inquiries and mail orders:
Finishing Line Press
PO Box 1626
Georgetown, Kentucky 40324
USA

Table of Contents

First Cut 1

Fearless 3

Victory Liquor and Lounge (2005) 5

Taco Tuesday 6

Permafrost 8

Buddleia Davidii 12

Former Champions 14

Screen Porch (after Dylan Thomas) 16

Cole Range (Army Ranger Assessment) 18

In This Polaroid 20

Meatless Monday 22

Glowing Embers 23

The First Time 24

Darby Range (Phase 1 of Army Ranger School) 25

Perfume 26

Senior Living 28

Tennis in the Time of Covid 29

Normal 31

The Things He Left Behind 33

Final Cut 35

First Cut

I take nothing for granted now,
neither the greening of
my glowing embers maple
nor the thorn from old-world rose;
instead, I judge the hickory's age
only when I count its rings.

Daphne, my backyard girlfriend,
our winter intimacy has passed,
though your anise-scented fragrance
lingers like perfume on a pillow,
and sweet camelia, you have unraveled,
your petals torn and shorn
like nylons and other wispy bits
dribbled across a bedroom floor.

But here come red bud and quince,
like twenty-somethings,
resplendent in their delicacy,
confident in their immortality,
and purple peony, thrusting lusty
through red clay and mulch,
daffodil and gentle clematis, too;
I welcome each in their time,
say their names aloud,
and ask them to remember me
when the bloom is off their faces
and they lie again in unmarked graves.

And here's to the first cut
of spring's nascent lawn,
fallen victim over winter
to henbit and deadnettle,
speedwell, groundsel, and wild garlic;
and here's to the Honda's blade
that beheads those bastards and
banishes their body-bagged remains to the curb.

And also raise a glass to Scott's Weed and Feed,
guaranteed to fertilize fine fescue and Kentucky blue,
certified to defeat wild violet, ground ivy,

plantain, and lespedeza
in one replenishing and lethal dose.
But I take nothing for granted now,
neither the squirrel's journey, branch to branch,
nor the worm's turning of the soil;
instead, I remind myself that the air I swallow
today will visit distant stars tomorrow.

Fearless

I keep an old photo of my son
on a stand next to my bed,
a memory to remind me
of who he is when
I wake up thinking
about the velocity of bullets
and indifference of bombs.

We're on Pawley's Island
a few years back,
my boy's maybe nine or ten;
it's pastel time on a beach
white as a cotton field,
soft as two glasses of wine.

Clouds billow pink above,
while below, my son races a
foaming phalanx to shore,
bare chest thrust out,
arms outstretched,
blonde hair gleaming.

He's not worried about jellyfish
swimming the shallows,
has no concern for
the fisherman's hook,
rusty nail, or stingray slithering.

He's laughing. He's fearless.

He's the kid at the diner
who can't sit still,
the kid like a breakneck slide
down a Carolina waterfall,
like a handstand on the lip
of the Grand Canyon,
like a soldier
on the battlefield
moving low and fast
through the shrapnel storm.

I snap my pic before he turns
and bolts,
weaving through
twilight-passing strangers,
an open-field halfback
on a Saturday football field.

When I call his name,
he hears only wind,
but I wait until he's nearly
out of sight
before I take the chase.

Victory Liquor and Lounge (2005)

Come, you heroes of Victory
Liquor and Lounge,
grizzly-whiskered and silver-haired,
bitter-fingered and hard-lipped,
sitting your bar stools and
spinning your riff, sharing wrinkled
memories and outright lies,
over smoke from Chesterfields and Lucky Strikes,
dulled by whisky and beer, opioids, and crystal meth,
dissembled by unzipped flies and
bellies billowing above leather belts.

Come now, World War II and Korea,
Vietnam, Iraq, and Afghanistan;
come, Ford Motor and Western Union,
Johnson Controls and Holiday Rambler.

Praise be for Social Security, Medicare, and
prosthetic limbs; bless IRA, 401(k), and
the VA for a place to stay when minds
unwind and wounds once healed bleed anew.

Come now, you welders and butchers,
telephone linemen and railroaders,
middle managers and salesmen,
come, carpenters, plumbers, and preachers.

Remember the fallen of the Forty Second,
the rowdy Rangers of the Seventy Fifth,
the Screaming Eagles of the One O One,
the mean Marines of Alpha, Bravo, Charlie.

Remember the bosses on every line,
the overtime shifts that left you for dead,
the hirings and firings and lay-offs,
the promotions you should have had.

Come now, you beautiful boys of Victory,
you fathers and sons, husbands and brothers,
rest here at last on this distant shore,
your sacrifice and slaughter done.

Taco Tuesday

From your home office
I hear tap-tapping on your laptop,
catch bits of business conversation—
you work harder than you should.

I make a marinade that embraces
this week's meat, *carne asada* or *pollo,*
like you embraced me, naked and unafraid
on our stolen holiday in Ensenada.

Cilantro-lime rice steams, each grain
awaiting your taste. The sizzle of
sauteed onions and peppers in an iron
skillet, your fingertips on my skin.

Re-fried beans demand a stir, but not quite
the stir we made all those years ago. No one
gave us a gambler's chance—fleeing
first marriages, fourteen years between us.

You confessed on our first date
you didn't cook and didn't intend
to learn, as if that made a difference
to a man afire in his own grease.

This time of day it's pink-light and shadow,
and memory moves like my chef's knife—
the son who climbed the back-yard hickory,
the daughter who tried to take her life.

A passing cloud darkens the room before
slats of sunlight enliven dust motes again.
Now it's just the two of us; who knew
we'd make it to this final course?

So, I sear the meat like hearts seared
by the passage of time, marking tendon
and fat, charring skin. I season with chili
powder, cumin, and other secrets we share.

I work from scratch, kneading masa
for tortillas like I needed your breasts
the first time we lay together,
flesh to flesh, tequila to margarita.

When I call you to dinner,
your tapping slows to a halt—
I add a squeeze of lime for acid,
sprinkle cilantro to ground us to the earth.

Permafrost

Permafrost is thawing;
water frozen for ages
and holding together
the arctic's subterranean mosaic
of stone, gravel, and corpse
is melting,
leading to collapse, flooding, and the release
of ancient microbes and deadly viruses
into an already fragile atmosphere.

But this summer
my daughter turns forty
to my seventy,
the thirty years before
she arrived and the forty since
all I can count.

The night of her birth
she remained at the hospital
with my then wife
while I drove home,
stopping at a tavern
for a cold one
to relieve the stress
of witnessing childbirth
and the terror
and responsibility
that pressed down on my shoulders
like the weight of a gazillion tons
of ice and soil and sand.

When I related my situation
to the barkeep,
he said no worries,
my beer was free,
and three or four others,

older men who'd overheard,
emerged and also bought me beers,
saying congratulations,
welcome to the wonder of fatherhood.

It was great, the men assured me,
just great, make no mistake,
if I didn't mind poop
under my nails
and vomit
down the back of my shirt,
so long as I was good
with lack of sleep and sex
for months on end
and could accept my wife's
weight gain and the strain
on my wallet.

It's best, the men said
while they're still in diapers,
before the little shits
learn to walk through glass doors
and climb kitchen counters,
before they turn
into pre-teen drama queens
with erupting pimples,
and wet-dream penises,
before they mutate
into know-it-all teenagers
who won't listen to parents
any more than one extinct
mastodon listened to the next;
instead of respect,
the best I could expect
was a hot, steaming plate
of what can you do
for me next, Dad.

The bartender and tavern men,
I suppose they're dead, now,
their grinning skulls
awaiting discovery
by future generations
when their coffins
bob to the surface
of a rising ocean.

But that night of my daughter's birth
they breathed fire,
danced naked in moonlight;
just kidding,
they said winking
and slapping my back,
fatherhood is excellent,
really excellent;
here, have another beer,
you'll need it,
hardee har, har, har.

My daughter, a smart
and capable woman,
teaches English, now,
to the smartest kids in Omaha,
and with her decent,
capable husband
raises three children of her own,
well-behaved children,
the kind of children
who send grandpa fudge
and thank-you cards
at Christmas.

But this summer,
she'll turn forty,
and I'll be seventy,
all those years between
no more than a
glint of sunlight
off a liquifying glacier.

Awake at night,
I listen to the trickle,
the drip, drip. drip
of time's passing,
for thawing begets thawing,
allowing greenhouse gasses
to escape the earth's
subconsciousness,

seal in the heat of decay,
and encourage molecules
bound together for eons
to say their sweet goodbyes.

Buddleia Davidii

My butterfly bush
is stunning today
after I shaped her up,
after the rains came,
the sun now burning bright.

She's blooming violet
and attracting bees
and hummingbirds
like nobody's business—
it's her job, after all.

Yeah, she looks really good, today;
anyone can see she doesn't
care about Covid or racial unrest,
isn't concerned about Presidential
politics or unemployment rates.

She's in the upper one percent, today,
fully invested in Apple and Amazon,
today, with a house on the coast,
a cabin in the mountains, and
two shiny, new cars in the drive.

My butterfly bush is smiling
like a fresh-picked Early Girl
tomato, today, swaying in the
breeze like a Hawaiian hula babe,
hubba hubba, hubba hubba, hubba.

Yeah, she looks quite fine, today.
Ask the fresh-cut grass or
newly planted clematis,
as if they have an opinion
about buddleia davidii.

That's her real name, you know,
her Latin name, the name she wants
to be called when she's stretched out
naked on the bed,
panting across the pillow.

Budd leia   david ii.
Say it   whisper it.
Oh, yeah, she owns you,
and there's not a
damn thing you can do about it.

Former Champions

It's taken a while to acknowledge
your death except in dreams
in which we're climbing a mountain;
you reach for my hand,
then slip your grip and fall,
tumble one rock to the next
like an empty gin bottle
kicked down a two AM avenue.

I wake up knowing no one survives that,
and then try to remember how you were
before losing your grip, back when
we drank beer instead of gin and wine
and talked baseball and girls instead
of cratering careers and women,
before you started believing in Rush
and shooting pool with crooked cues.

Back when your smile made me feel
like laundry fresh off the line,
when you were shiny and bright
as a dime in the sun, strong and sure
as a chain link fence stretched across
a thousand acres of American prairie,
before your silver tarnished, your fence
fell down, and your cows ran mad.

We watched the aurora borealis
roar across an Indiana sky, survived a
white-out while driving to Chicago, and
fished Minnesota lakes so cold and blue
nuclear fusion couldn't melt their hearts.
So, it pissed me off when you lost your
fast ball and started throwing knucklers
that fluttered and floated outside the strike zone.

I can't say, exactly, which corporate reorg,
new boss, financial hardship, or transitional wife
dispensed you into the ditch, but I know
you eventually refused to look for work or
even get out of bed, and I heard you broke bread

with the homeless after your brother threatened
to kill you if you showed your sorry face again;
no one knew the name of your malaise.
No one expected this could happen
to you who, back in the day, piled up
awards and accolades like dirty dishes,
you who held your nerve when
others danced with sweaty hands,
clubbed feet, and fibrillating hearts,
you who made it look so damn easy
the rest of us believed we could do it, too.

Some guys offered money or
a sofa to sleep on. I wrote letters
and e-mails, and tried calling until
you took yourself out of the game
and left the stadium early,
before we resolved, once and for all,
who owned the sweeter swing, Musial or Clemente,
before we decided the better fighter, Ali or Smokin' Joe.

Some redwood giants perish
as saplings, their promise unfulfilled,
and some boys remain little league forever,
unwilling or unable to play the Bigs;
some guys putt the long green with
expensive and overwrought clubs;
some guys choose the ole *Billy Baroo;
some guys roll boulders and blow the blues.

---

*Name of the famous putter used in the final scene of the 1980 film starring Bill Murray, *Caddyshack*

Screen Porch (after Dylan Thomas)

Early Sunday morning, and
the boys across the street
have been kicked to the curb
where they play easy in the sun,
happy as the grass is green,
too high octane to remain
inside while parents sleep
or make love lazy and free
or drowse peaceful and quiet
in the amber glow of simple light.

The brothers swat down a spider's
web stretched across the porch,
shoot hoops and play baseball,
ride bicycles and chase snakes,
golden in the mercy of the sun,
carefree as pebbles in a stream,
yet all the while trading accusations,
threatening reprisals, and crying
out loud because a soccer ball
has rolled down a sewer drain.

I don't mind their noise
for I once was those boys,
happy and green and famous
among the backyard apple trees,
honored by the cherry and mulberry,
barefoot destroyer of spiders' webs
laced like doilies across our dew-wet lawn,
star of garage hoop championships,
and keeper of the chicken coop threatened
by weasels scheming in the dusky wood.

And I once was those parents,
singing to my horn and tethered
to my money wheel sixty hours a week,
imprisoned behind office windows
in a cage of glass and steel,
anxious as the day is long,
and prince of dirty diapers,
nighttime nippled bottles,

baby books, pink and purple
unicorns and braying Little Ponies.
Now, time has taken me by the hand,
led me to this screen porch, and
seated me in this rocking chair,
fled forever from my childhood,
where I once was young and easy in his means,
when the days stretched long as the
moon's journey across the star-scarred sky;
easy now in my easy chair I listen to
the boys laughing in their fields of praise.

Cole Range (Army Ranger Assessment)

Lack of sleep, food, and water
triggers hallucinations

like the one claimed by my son
during Ranger assessment

on a night he maneuvered alone
with only a compass and a map.

Lost in a thicket of southern
pine, exhaustion, and self-doubt,

he imagined me, dressed in jeans
and flannel shirt, leaning into his world,

urging him on like a cue ball
urges the eight into the pocket.

Although sleep was forbidden,
he slept ten minutes, no more,

while I stood guard,
like when he was a little boy.

But when he awoke, I'd left him
to complete his mission alone.

I don't believe in God unless
god is but another word for unknown.

I don't believe in ghosts unless
despair is but the ghost of hope.

But I know old men lie awake
at night, misgivings accumulating

like debris on tumbleweed
blown across a prairie scape.

And I know a son is father
to the father of the son

no less than the earth is
father to the moon.

In This Polaroid

taken by an off-stage actor
my mother's drive-way peonies
have fallen face-down like
spring-breakers on a sandy beach.

Her begonias sunbathe beside
the little, yellow house that knew
our hearts by heart and recited our dreams
in its sleep while we lay in bed waiting
for the Indiana day to begin.

My father sits legs crossed
beneath the purple pansy baskets,
there in his plastic patio chair,
looking like a trailer court king
set upon his throne.

Well, he was king of the charcoal grill
grinning behind him and the cutting room
at Wilt's Super Mart where he and his boys
butchered beef quarters into steaks and chops
for a half-decent living.

He holds an anxious amber drink
in his right hand, thick, black brows
stenciled above eyes intense as a storm
brewing over a Florida gulf he's never been to,
and a facial expression that instead of a smile
is one of concern; to be fair, he pulled
behind his engine a mortgage, a car payment,
and two kids and a wife who wanted a
Lauderdale spring break like whiskey wants water.

It's 1967 and his Cards are on a pennant run
the winning of which he's bet more on
than he can afford to lose.

He's listening to their double header
on a transistor radio that sizzles
like his momma's bacon in her
dust bowl frying pan; maybe,

Gibby's fast ball will strike out another batter,
or Brock steal another base,
or Maris clock another homerun.
What is time that it can stop on this dime,
yet stretch there to here like baseball bubble gum
and, finally, fold itself into a favored family photograph.

Meatless Monday

I invite zucchini, squash, and okra
to this party, sautéing in butter
to create texture and color.

They say this is good for us,
lowers blood pressure and cholesterol,
but we've never been good about what's good for us.

I season with salt, curry, and cayenne
for veg are bland, comprised only of water
and an allusion to the soil in which they grew.

But baby, you and I are carnivores, preferring flavors
of copper and iron, our union born of blood and bone
and rendered in fat and muscle.

We left our green and leafy past
flattened by the road to feast at a table
set with all manner of beast.

We embrace flame, eat what we kill or catch,
and have been known to slather our bodies
with marrow before licking the other clean.

It's Meatless Monday, and quinoa sometimes
tags along; kale, cauliflower, or broccolini
could also make the scene.

But you and I are carnivores,
preferring the sear and sizzle
of beef, bison, or fowl over
vegetables in a jumble.

Glowing Embers

My Japanese maple tree
has waited all year for
this clear autumn morning.

Last week's hurricane
brought wind and rain
but left her unscathed.

Better off than her neighbor,
the brugmansia vine that toppled
and now refuses to climb.

Better off, too, than Mr. Hickory
who lost his nuts and nerve
and now presents as a pencil.

Unlike them, Miss Glowing Embers
celebrates with leaves of yellow and
orange, a hint of red around the edges.

She's telling the squirrel
he's welcome to play.

She's offering the sparrow
a branch on which to rest.

She's anchoring the spider's web
without complaint or trepidation.

She's singing, if you want the truth,
doing a little dance before the
first frost freezes in a day or two.

She never sees it coming,
never expects this, her moment,
and never anticipates its end.

The First Time

my mother slapped my face,
causing cheeks and lips
to sizzle
like she'd flicked
hot grease from a skillet,
I had it coming
for teasing the sisters
who lived in the shanty
behind Bailey's store.

Slapped for deriding dresses
sewn from patchwork scraps,
dresses with missing buttons,
hems frostbit by ice and snow,
sleeves like stovepipes,
and waists bunched
and belted by string.

Slapped across the face
for teasing dresses
about the same as those
made from flour sacks
by my Granny for my
mother when my mother
was the sisters' age
and they lived on the
cotton farm next to the
tracks where trains
split the night like
an axe splitting wood.

Slapped into a six-year old's
shame for a tease
I've owned all these years
but maybe slapped also
for a tease I couldn't own,
a tease received
before I was born.

Darby Range (Phase 1 of Army Ranger School)

First week on Darby Range,
and there's a cold snap like
the snap of Granny's willow
switch across my bare ass.

For sassing or swearing or
refusing to dress against
autumn's first fallen snow
before slipping out the door.

First week on Darby Range
for my Army Airborne Ranger,
and there's a front coming in,
cold as a dead man's kiss.

Or the spray off Lake Michigan
hitting the breakwater in December
or the slush that gathers in boots
while shoveling the driveway.

First week of Ranger School,
and I bet my boy would enjoy
a cup of Granny's hot chocolate,
or a bite of her buttermilk biscuit.

Dipped in red-eye gravy and
served with a side of ham
or buttered up and sweetened
with a dab of homemade jam.

First week on Darby Range
and Rangers practice The Kill,
slicing like scythes through
wheat among tall Georgia pine.

Lean as blades forged in flame,
Army Airborne Rangers
prefer heat to cold,
would rather burn than freeze.

Perfume

I once witnessed a woman run naked
from a house, like a sunny-side-
up egg yolk running across a plate.

Sturdy and fragile at the same time,
she dashed past, hard, lean muscles
gleaming white beneath a streetlight.

Wearing only her Covid mask, she
trailed a fragrance reminiscent of a
perfume my ex-wife used to wear.

The man she'd bolted from stood in
his doorway, also naked, looking like
a fat gerbil whose treadmill has broken.

He held a wisp of clothes in one
hand and asked from behind his
homemade mask if I'd seen her.

About so high, he said, about yay
big around, he motioned, maybe
naked or nearly so, he noted.

My ex-wife's family owned an
apple orchard, and the barn where
they pressed cider smelled of the

essence of apples, sweet and
musky, pungent and ripe. But
she was not the kind of woman

who made love in an apple
barn or under an apple tree, and
surely not the kind of woman

who ran naked in the night or
called naked from a doorway
or wandered dark streets alone.

And I pretended for as long as I
could that I was not the kind of man
who wanted to run naked in broad
daylight, like a clear, clean mountain
stream teaming with trout with wide
open mouths and untamed hearts.

I'm not even sure anymore
where she lives, what perfume
she wears, or who she's married to.

From behind my own mask, I told
the man in the doorway I'd seen
nothing, and he said all he'd wanted

was to kiss her, a real kiss, lips on lips,
maybe a little tongue, he was so tired
of trying to be someone he wasn't.

Senior Living

See how soft the light,
I ask the TV man
for there's no one
else to listen.

See how soft the light,
now that the storm has passed.

I've worn PJs
all day and carried
coffee in a cup
one end to the other.

Next door doesn't care;
he's in his underwear,
jaw hanging loose
as a cellar door.

The attendant rolls him away
when he begins to pray.

She lives on a farm,
raising hogs prized for their cuts,
her mouth turned up,
a scythe when she smiles.

We should be clean
after all this rain,
thunder, and lightning,
clean as a razor's nick.

We should be new
as toys under
a Christmas tree cut
from a virgin field.

But do you hear the nightingale,
I ask the TV man

Tennis in the Time of Covid

Four old men take the tennis court,
more resembling fat barristers
than athletes.

See how they flail about, more
like drunken ballet dancers
than racqueteers.

See how they maintain a safe and social
distance, even when they should close
the net together.

See how they racquet tap or fist bump
for safety's sake following a
well-played point.

See how they sometimes neglect safety
in favor of a crease of shade
during changeovers.

They're old and forgetful, and Covid,
this uninvited guest, was not
expected so late to the party.

Their aging, at-risk bodies harbor
cancer, bad tickers, and fatty,
cirrhotic livers.

Their wives swept them out the door this
morning like dust bunnies, saying
have fun with the boys, honey.

Their wives wish for a time not so long
ago when husbands weren't dust
bunnies gathering at their feet.

See how they rally from the base
line, volley in the service box,
and lob when in doubt.

The defensive lob is their shot
of choice on nearly every
contested point.

Four old men take the tennis court,
more resembling folding chairs
than athletes.

Normal

What if cell phones, Netflix,
harnessed electricity, and
Atlantic City are but dusty bits
swept up in a slippery wind?

What if banking, commerce,
crypto currency, and haute
cuisine amount to less than
last week's forgotten dreams?

Remember, moons orbiting
various worlds, sentries on task,
are mere anomalies in the
galaxy's greater scheme.

And our Earth twirled and lurked
in empty space for nearly one
billion years, a sere and fallow
turd on a rapidly expanding plane

before the first volcano belched,
before the Great Oxygenation
Event birthed mitochondria,
DNA, and eukaryotic cells.

Bacteria have thrived for
three point two billion years.
Dinosaurs called the shots for a
period of time measured in eons.

Humankind made the scene only
a few thousand years ago, most
of our history endured in hovels,
no running water, heat, or AC,

our well-being exposed to
disease and pestilence, our daily
routines reduced to quarrels over
ragged pieces of animal hide.

So, maybe, Normal is living
in fear and cringing at
every twig broken beyond
the boma's protective wall.

Maybe, Normal is the sound of
a black hole sucking the Milky
Way in behind it before both
dive into another dimension.

Maybe, Normal is a tiny virus
silently exposing our hubris
and closing the book on the
next chapter of our whatever.

The Things He Left Behind

Candy wrappers winking from beneath the bed,
sheets and blankets in a twisted tangle,
pillows stacked like building blocks.

Baseball caps and faded family photographs,
Tin Tin collectibles and athletic medals,
plastic soldiers napping in a cabinet.

A ruck pack filled with sixty pounds of stones,
a fourth-grade book report for Miss York,
a Brooks Brothers' blazer, once worn.

Picture books of back-hoes, tractors and trucks,
six months of pay stubs from Pizza Hut,
some semi-automatic weapons' mags.

A few angry holes punched though hallway walls,
uncounted scars etched on girlfriends' hearts.
a six-pack of Coors in an outside fridge.

A backyard deer-stand, leaning on a tree,
one old black dog that doesn't care,
another that pines for his return.

A high school diploma, hard-earned,
tennis racquets and tumbling mats,
an electric piano, rarely played.

A bike, a trike, and much-liked skateboard,
a rock climber's helmet, well-used,
a tent for camping in the woods.

Beachball, soccer ball, softball, basketball, and football,
weightlifting equipment and fifty-pound weights,
a leather bag filled with pretty little marbles.

A would-be parachute for leaping off the roof,
cowboy cap pistols that no longer shoot,
water wings, kayaks, and inner tubes.

Pens and pencils that refuse to write,
algebra worksheets, incomplete,
a note to self to concentrate.

Final Cut

Before the reaper takes his final cut,
whether by the scythe's silent sweep
or the Honda's fatal roar,
there's so much to be done.

So much to be done as days narrow
to slivers chipped from onyx stone
and nights widen into dark rivers
rolling sleepless and uneasy to the sea.

Dry leaves and thatch must be raked and
left neat for the undertaker at the curb,
bare soil must be scored by hand or
aerated if you can afford the cost.

But nothing is without cost,
not seed sewn in bare patches,
fertilizer dearly applied, or
bad decisions made in spring.

Affairs must be placed in order,
wheat winnowed from chaff,
farewells made and scores settled,
the scarecrow laid at last to rest.

The clinging tomatoes will be sauced,
beans and okra picked and canned,
sweet basil's codicil will be drawn,
her last will and testament done.

All occurs in its turn as a wedding
suit becomes a dead man's clothes,
as a child born in March lies down
in mid-December's grave.

Gary V. Powell, a retired lawyer, lives with his beautiful wife and two intrepid dogs near the shores of lovely Lake Norman, North Carolina. A nominee for Pushcart and O'Henry prizes, a 2023 deGroot Foundation Writer of Note, winner of the 2022 Press 53/Prime Number Fiction Prize, and a finalist or honorable mention for numerous other fiction awards, his work appears or is forthcoming in *Carvezine, The Thomas Wolfe Review, The North Carolina Literary Review, Ocotillo Review, Prime Number, Atticus Review, Smokelong Quarterly, Best New Writing 2015,* and *Sleep is a Beautiful Color: the 2017 National Flash Fiction Day Anthology.* His chapbook, *Super Blood Wolf Moon,* won Kallisto Gaia Press's 2020 Contemporary Poetry Prize; more recent poetry appears or is forthcoming in *Main Street Rag, the San Diego Poetry Annual, Kakalak 2022,* and *Southword 2023.*

www.ingramcontent.com/pod-product-compliance
Lightning Source LLC
Chambersburg PA
CBHW022123090426
42743CB00008B/980